MORE
CONVERSATIONS
WITH THE AWAKENER

BAL NATU

1993

Sheriar Foundation

Copyright © 1993 Sheriar Foundation.

All rights reserved.

Printed in the U.S.A. by Sheriar Press, Inc.

Cover photograph: Copyright © FPG International/Larry West. Used by permission.

No part of this book may be reproduced, stored in a retrieval system, or transmitted in any form or by any means, electronic, mechanical, photocopy, recording, or otherwise without prior written permission of the publisher, except by a reviewer who wishes to quote brief passages in connection with a review written for inclusion in a magazine, newspaper, or broadcast. For information write: Sheriar Foundation, 3005 Highway 17 North Bypass, Myrtle Beach, South Carolina 29577, U.S.A.

ISBN: 1-880619-07-5

Dedicated to You
The Awakener
of
All Hearts
and to
All those who are seeking You
Honestly and wholeheartedly.

Benediction astounding;
Benevolence amazing!

Beyond words, beyond silence,
Awakened Awareness are You;
Balancing creation by Your Presence,
Accept this offering unto You.

Contents

- iii   Dedication
- vii   Preamble
- 1   Drops of Your Presence
- 3   Don't Be Too Long
- 9   Incredible Moments of Bliss
- 14   Prayer – An Intimate Dialogue with You
- 20   Personality, Individuality, and Reality
- 28   The Perfect Timing
- 31   You Alone Are Mine
- 38   Bathing One's Being
- 44   Let a Sip Be a Celebration!
- 50   Remember Me Full-Heartedly
- 52   A Cosmic Call
- 61   Influence, Presence, and Essence
- 70   Just for Nothing
- 75   The Book
- 83   The Bill Unpayable
- 89   The Gifts
- 95   Inseparable Are Your Name and Form

Preamble

*A Conversation with You,
and the Readers*

You are the Reality; I am a little nothing in You.
However, in Your unconditional love,
You have designed a way most natural for me to come
    closer to You.
It's a sort of private avenue where I can stop anywhere
and have an intimate dialogue with You on any subject.
I am beholden to You for this gift of a solitary route,
leading me closer to You.

For me, our brief dialogues are always
rich in significance, and exhilarating.
To others, they may be meaningful, or meaningless.

The conversations compiled here are the dim reflections
gathered by me of what I "said" and what You "said."

But I must admit that in many instances, I might have missed
or misunderstood or perhaps misrepresented
some of Your profound statements.
Even where I have succeeded, however
words do have their own limits; they are only indicators.
Here, I am reminded of the following incident:

Once I knocked on Your door and asked, "Are You in?"
You softly laughed and said, "I am not inside!"
Your repartee was a unique blending of a true and false reply,
laced with Your humor.
It also expressed, simultaneously, the utility and futility of words.
You are at times so subtle that it is not easy to know what You mean.

So, dear readers, these conversations
may bemuse you or amuse you,
may shock you or surprise you,
but believe me, I don't mean to bore you.

Salutations to You,
thanks to my dear companions,
and welcome to the readers.

Bal Natu

Drops of Your Presence

I approached You and asked, "Do You know what they say about *Conversations?*"

"What? I am omniscient, yet I do not know anything about this!" And You chuckled.

"When anyone likes any of the conversations, the person comes to me with a look of surprise and suspicion and whispers to me, 'Did you write that? Who wrote it?' "

"So what's your reply?"

"Simple. Not me!"

"Then who?"

"I do not know."

"Why do you say that?"

"What else should I answer?"

"Well, you have to figure it out." And Your omniscient eyes pierced me.

"Oh, now I know. The moment You wished it, I got it."

"Amazing!" And You asked eagerly, "What's the answer?"

"It's not me; it's not anyone else; it's not You!"

"Strange!"

"Yes, it's strange, rare, but certainly true."

"What do you mean by this?"

"Well, whenever You graciously pull me into the ocean of Your being, the moment I come out, drops of Your presence falling on the beach form these conversations. So they are mine, yet not mine."

Your eyes sparkled merrily, and You pinched my ear. "Clever!" And the ripples of Your lively laughter engulfed us and drowned me in Your wordless presence.

– In response to letters from readers
of the author's earlier book,
Conversations with The Awakener.

Don't Be Too Long

Morning broke softly, breezes blew merrily through the fields, and as I was walking leisurely down a secluded road, a celestial hush was in the air. A deep quietude seemed to prevail over earth and sky.

Then something unexpected happened: You appeared from a path that cut through the swaying green crops. Radiating a warm smile, You joined me on my walk.

This was amazing! Although I have talked with You often, I had never before walked with You, keeping step and feeling the rhythm of Your gait. What a profound and novel experience! A feeling of overwhelming wonderment bathed my being. I couldn't tell if I was walking on earth or in the heavens.

I do not recall how long we walked together without speaking. Finally You asked me teasingly, "Are you observing silence today?" And this brought me down to earth.

"No, no," I replied. "But why don't we go to that rocky knoll and talk there?"

Happily, You agreed, so we climbed the knoll and sat down. Not finding myself in a mood for conversation, and needing more time to adjust to the sweet shock of Your unexpected arrival, I remarked casually on the beauty of the sunrise. "Isn't it fascinating how the sun is mirrored in the leaves, shimmering in everything?"

In appreciation of my observation, You looked at the horizon, but did not seem much impressed. "Wonderful reflections depicting marvelous, imperfect shades of light. However, know well that I alone am the perfect Mirror."

Intrigued, in spite of myself, for I still wasn't ready for a serious or weighty discussion, I asked, "What do You mean by this?"

"I mean that I am so immaculately clean and impressionless that I reflect fully and clearly what you are, as you are. This presents a challenge and also an opportunity for you, or anyone."

"What is that challenge?"

"That you dare to accept this with neither self-justification nor self-condemnation."

"And the opportunity?"

"That I shall gladly lead you on to what you should be."

"What is that?"

"Another mirror."

"But how is this possible?"

"Don't ask Me how. It is not that I do not wish to tell you, but just hearing the words will not, in itself, be of any benefit to you. On the contrary, it may even harm you."

I was perplexed. "But why?"

"Because the process of cleansing away the images on the mirror is at times delightful, and at times painful."

"Can't You help me to avoid the painful parts?" I asked impatiently.

"Not entirely. You see, you have formed many respectable, rigid images of yourself; they are deeply engraved on your mind and heart. These, in turn, are shielded by many layers of thoughts and self-centered feelings. So, ironically, in your quest for freedom, you have caged yourself more and more, and deviated farther from your real Nature."

"I fear I have not fully followed You. Confused as I am, my question has become more complicated by Your answer. Sorry. Please confuse me only as much as I can bear."

"What you can easily bear is no confusion!"

"Now my confusion is even worse!"

"When confusion is tired of itself, it becomes clarity," You said, and smiled. "But what is basically wrong with confusion?"

"What's good about it? Does confusion serve some specific, vital purpose in my life?"

"Yes, of course. But only from the moment you have offered yourself willingly to Me. Then confusion opens a new dimension in your life."

"I am amazed to hear this!" I responded.

"What is there to be amazed about? In confusion, you feel tired of yourself, and so you call on Me, more and more, to take over the situation. On the other hand, in the state of so-called clarity, you cling more tightly to the image of yourself, which results in a stalemate in your journey to Me – the eternally Impressionless One – and you continue to go in circles in the whirlpool of your imagined ideal."

"Then do you want me to be in a state of confusion rather than clarity?"

"No. You have missed the real point. What counts is neither confusion nor clarity, but greater and deeper trust in Me – trust in My being with you all the time, whatever state you are in."

A small cloud can eclipse the sun. At that moment a passing thought veiled my mind and heart; I suddenly remembered that I was due to meet a friend. Against my will, anxiety began to darken my appreciation of Your sunlit words. Strange but true! Incredible are the ways of self to fortify itself.

Abruptly I said, "I am expecting a dear friend of mine to visit me this morning. I haven't seen him for many months."

The expression on Your face changed. Gently, You replied, "Really? Why didn't you tell Me sooner?" And, apologetically, You added, "Sorry I kept you so long. I won't delay you further."

With these words You reached over and patted my shoulder. "Go, go home quickly, otherwise you might not be there to welcome your friend."

I got up and began to walk fast toward the house. A petty, fleeting bond of affection – a passing cloud blocking the sun – made me even forget to say goodbye.

My friend did not come that morning, nor even that week. This made me think all the more about the loss of Your company, and my own stupidity with You. I would not have imagined that a trivial relationship could be so illusive and possessive as to draw me away from You, the most Intimate One. Surely on that day I most foolishly traded the perfect Mirror for a piece of shining glass.

Whenever I recall the guileless expression on Your face as You said, "Sorry, " with that genuine intimacy, it pains my heart. I marvel at Your unconditional love that flows in spite of my repeatedly foolish behavior.

Weeks have now passed, and sometimes I go out for morning walks. The outside, visible world remains as lovely as ever, but it holds no charm for me. It is now devoid of something vital – the warmth of Your company, which I belittled, and even dishonored.

Now, let every step I take be an invitation to You. Please visit me, even for a few moments, so that I may confess my folly to You and beg Your pardon. Until then, normalcy shall not return to my life. My grief is becoming poignant. This pain of longing is also Your gift, and I know You will come. But when? Come soon. Don't be too long.

Incredible Moments of Bliss

One quiet night I strolled along the seashore beneath a star-studded sky. Overwhelmed by the immensity of space and galaxies, I laid myself down on the sand, staring upward, wondering at this ever-renewing phenomenon. The awesome panorama stilled my mind, opened my heart, and for some moments an indescribable bliss filled my being.

However, the bliss left me as suddenly as it came, and I found myself in a bottomless contemplation: Does this stupendous enormity continue to stretch forth in all directions without end? Is it just one purposeless, passive awareness, extending itself to infinity, or is it an active consciousness, threading through all that seems to exist?

Is a great incomprehensible disorder swallowing all lesser orders? Or is there a prodigious, unexplored order silently directing all apparent disorders under which the dreams of millions of people and billions of creatures flower and wither, to blossom again?

Fantastic!

I felt I could not contain within myself the magnitude and mystery of it all. Ecstatic, I leaped to my feet, raised my hands, and danced and shouted at the top of my voice, "Incomprehensible! Incredible!"

A sweet, loving voice spoke behind me: "What is incredible?"

I turned and saw You smiling at me with a mischievous glint in Your eye.

Startled though I was, I burst out laughing. "Your being here, at this moment, is super-incredible!"

Then we laughed together, and sat down on the sand.

Surveying my awestruck, bemused expression, You asked me if I was feeling all right. I shook my head and mumbled, "Not quite, until I hear something from you."

"About what?"

"About those rapturous moments I just experienced. Where did they come from, and where have they gone?"

"They receded to where they came from."

I frowned in mock gravity and said, "Don't make fun of my question. I'm serious."

Your eyes glimmered, and You answered me, "I am

absolutely serious. These moments visit anyone when body, mind, and heart are in harmony, and when no expectations exist. Then this nameless wonder, contained within this universal mystery, opens up and bliss spills out. To live even for a moment in this wonder is to renew one's being in My presence."

"This is still enigmatic. What does this harmony You speak of mean?"

"It means what it means."

"You seem to be in a humorous mood today. But please let Your answer be comprehensible."

Your expression turned serious as You gazed at me. "I have no answer that will fit your rational comprehension. But try to listen carefully to what I say. The Source of bliss is ever-present within you. As soon as your thoughts and feelings offer no resistance, there is harmony, and bliss flows forth. But these moments recede with the first surge of possessiveness, for they are extremely pure, and extremely shy.

"Any moment is what you make it," You continued. "Its meaning depends upon how you respond to it, and how you let it happen. It can be active or passive or simply silent; it can be fast or slow, or an eternity. Perfect harmony is the harbinger of My pure presence. Are you listening to what I'm saying?"

My blank expression must have given me away. "I

am listening, but not following," I confessed. "Hearing music does not imply the ability to skillfully play an instrument. To be honest, everything You said just now is beyond my conception."

"It is the conception itself that you have to let go," You replied.

"I mean to say that I know the dictionary meanings of the words You use, but when these words form a sentence, it makes no sense to me. Perhaps my attempt to draw a specific meaning from Your statements conditions the unconditional game You play as the Lawless Infinite."

"Yes," You nodded. "That you see this much shows that your mind and heart are opening to the harmony within you. All the immensity of space is nothing compared to the immensity of silence that is within you. The rhythm of My remembrance drowns you in that silence which invites Me. These moments of bliss are the forerunners of My presence. Do you understand My words?"

I had to admit that I did not, quite. However, they struck an endearing chord in my heart. I looked into your deep-set eyes, which held eternity in them, and I heard You ask me, "Any question?"

Fairly dazed, I answered, "Question! What question? No questions!"

Again I saw that mischievous smile. And then You were gone.

Your disappearance seemed as natural as Your appearance. Yet Your arrival and departure were so astounding that it took me some time to come out of the spell they cast upon me. Then, as I returned to my normal senses, and became aware once again of the vast panorama, I wondered if Your visit had been only a projection of my own mind. But the next moment I heard a clear whisper from the heart, "No." And Your playful smile came back to me – a reminder not to be snared by the tricks of mind.

With an overwhelming sense of gratitude, I got up, looked up, closed my eyes, and the waves of deep silence rolled and resounded within me.

"Incomprehensible! Incredible!"

Prayer – An Intimate Dialogue with You

It was a holiday, and I wanted to make it a real "holy day" by offering prayers, meditating, and reading spiritual books. The day began well, very well. In the morning I had a nice bath and put on clean, loose clothes. Incense filled the room. I closed the door and solemnly stood up to pray.

Barely a few minutes had passed when I heard a knock at the door. A little annoyed, I opened the door to find one of my friends with a broad smile on his face. "Just came by to let you know that I'm going out to the country this weekend," he said.

I forced myself to be polite. "Thank you for telling me. Have a good time. Bye!" I closed the door and my smile melted. I resumed my prayer, trying to recompose myself.

A few minutes later, the phone rang. Again annoyed, I answered it brusquely. "Hello," I said.

"Oh," said the caller, "I'm sorry; wrong number," and hung up.

Although these interruptions irritated me, I somehow managed to finish my prayer. But now my plans for a day of peaceful reading and prayer seemed meaningless because of the dark mood that had settled in.

On the spur of the moment, I thought of doing something very mundane and down to earth. I decided to dust and rearrange the things given to me over the years by my friends and relatives. Soon a table was strewn with many things which awakened nostalgic memories from my past. I was handling a pouch of marbles given to me by my mother when I was a boy. Suddenly the cord came untied and the pouch burst open. Marbles bounced off in all directions. I went down on all fours, trying to gather them together again, when You patted me on the shoulder from behind, saying, "Here's one."

I looked at You and took the brilliant green marble that You held out to me. But I didn't speak a word, not even a "thank you."

"My, what a fine holiday mood you're in," You said with a twinkle in Your eye.

In spite of Your presence I couldn't get over my mood. I grimly responded, "I propose and You dispose!"

"Is that so?" You said, raising a questioning eyebrow. "Tell me what happened."

I narrated the incidents of the morning: my plans for a quiet time of spiritual reading and especially prayers, and the unexpected disturbances.

Looking straight into my eyes, You said, "But why do you separate your everyday living from a contemplative life?"

Without grasping the import of Your statement, I persisted, "Shouldn't I set aside some time for prayers and meditation?"

"Who says no? Have your plans. Sure. But offer them to My pleasure, and this will easily take away the pride of fulfilling your plans. Prayer should be a way to experiment and experience that whatever is happening is My wish."

"My mind is still muddled, and I don't follow what You said. Please explain a little more."

"Here is a figure. When someone is working on a spinning wheel, if the thread snaps, the person simply adds a little extra bit of cotton to join the fiber, and on goes the spinning. Haven't you noticed this?"

"Yes, I have. But its application in life doesn't seem so simple!"

"Presuppositions always make things more difficult. When the thread of your plans is broken, take a little bit of your trust in My wish to join the broken thread with the fibers that continue to spin off from life's wheel. Be open; be positive."

I looked at You. Your nearness seemed a blessing. And Your presence began to unfold its liveliness within me. How mistaken I'd been in being so annoyed by the disturbances this morning! I maintained a modest silence.

With eyes beaming, You continued, "Prayer should close the distance between you and Me. In prayer, you have to leave your self behind, making way for Me; you have to willingly disown your self so that I can enter all aspects of your life. It should be a joyous, voluntary grounding in My enlivening presence."

At this point, I interrupted, "But for a novice like me, surely a quiet atmosphere and a special time is helpful. Shouldn't I try to arrange such a setting?" In fact I was still trying to justify my earlier annoyance.

You gave me an amused and tolerant look and said, "There's nothing wrong in expecting or planning. But if things happen differently, you shouldn't be enraged. There are numberless factors working. And prayer should help you to respond to the changing situations around you from a place of poise within yourself. It becomes a wonderful game, when practice has made you a skilled player."

"Is there some technique or a special way to get to the center of poise within me?"

"There is and there isn't. It unfolds on its own when your prayers are offered with a warm heart. Just words alone don't constitute prayer. Rigidity can turn sublime words into rituals, while a sense of humor with discrimination can fill a prayer with liveliness. In that case, although the words remain the same, the prayer becomes alive, animated. Such prayers may be experienced at set times, or spontaneously any time in the course of daily life."

"Are there any clues that would help me to live such a life?"

"Many. But there is no set system to it. The more you 'catch' them, the more there are for you to 'catch'! But remember," You said in a mild tone, "there is one prerequisite: resign yourself to My wish with a cheerful heart. This will lead you to experience life as an integral whole without picking so many holes in it."

I saw the twinkle in Your eye and smiled sheepishly, remembering my foolish behavior that morning.

You continued, "You are just a drop in the Ocean that I am. When that 'dropness' becomes transparent through self-giving prayers, My Oceanic nature flows out through your veins, revitalizing your cells and releasing the glow of joy in your heart."

Just then the phone rang again. I picked it up and said, "Hello?" Then I put it down.

"What was it?" You asked.

"Wrong number," I said, then smiled.

"Well, that seems to be just the right note to ring in your new adventure. Remember: the real holiday is when you let go of 'self' so that I can be present in your life. Good luck!"

And the next moment I found myself alone in my room. Suddenly I realized that during the entire conversation, both of us were standing by that table with so many things strewn on it. In the midst of that chaos I had forgotten to offer You a seat.

Many a time I have noticed that in Your presence I lose my common sense. But each time, the profundity, humor, and wonder of the moments spent in Your company turn a light on inside me. This time, I gathered that each prayer is an intimate dialogue with You, encompassing all aspects of life. And that You are ready to respond anytime with a welcoming smile.

Personality, Individuality, and Reality

"May I tell You a story?" I asked You one day.

"How nice! I would be delighted to hear a story instead of answering questions!" And Your countenance glowed with a mischievous smile.

"Well, the questions may come later," I cautioned.

"Anyway, this is a good change, and I am fond of stories."

I gathered my wits, cleared my throat, and began:

"Once upon a time there lived a clown. He became very popular because when people attended his performances, they forgot their troubles and felt light-hearted. Everyone praised the curative powers of the laughter the clown was able to induce, and his shows were always sold out.

"Yet the irony was that the clown himself was sinking deeper and deeper into personal despair, as he was unable to face the challenges of his own life.

"Finally, at the end of his rope, he paid a visit incognito to a renowned psychologist. After hearing his problems in detail, the psychologist said, 'I strongly advise you to attend some performances by the famous clown who is currently on tour here in our city.'

"'But I am that clown!' the patient exclaimed.

"Even though the psychologist was an expert on every kind of human quirk, he got such a shock from this unforeseen turn of events that he swooned in his chair. He had helped many persons recover from their traumas, yet this forthright reply overwhelmed him.

"The clown took a bottle of smelling salts and set about reviving the distinguished psychologist. What a comical tragedy! The clown began saying softly, 'Sir, I am okay. Please don't worry about me. Come back to your senses. You are in your own consulting room'.

"The psychologist soon revived, and the clown left the doctor's office. But as he came out, he was struck with the realization that he would have to seek the answer to his problems from another source, deeper than psychology.

"And, as far as I know," I concluded, "that's the end of the story. I don't know what happened after that."

And I looked at You to see Your reaction.

With a serious look, You answered, "The wounds

of the heart are not totally healed by the sciences of the mind."

I gazed at You thoughtfully and said, "Life is so ironic, such a quizzical joke! It makes me wonder how I can adapt my personality to face all the bizarre situations that come up in life. To be frank, I do not know what 'personality' really is, or how it can be effectively molded."

With a sympathetic tenderness, You responded, "First ask yourself whether you are ready to come out of the identity in which you have caged yourself"

"Yes, I wish to be free, but I don't know how."

"I will help you when you are one hundred percent willing."

"I'm afraid that's asking too much of me," I replied. "Could we start with one percent?"

You smiled and said, "Okay. But in this one percent you should be one hundred percent sincere."

"Believe me, to the extent that I know, I am."

"You want to know what this 'personality' is."

"Yes!" I said eagerly.

"But do you realize what a deep and subtle question it is?"

"Not really. But today, while conversing with You, this word which I have heard so many times just popped into my head."

Personality, Individuality, and Reality

"Then pay attention to what I say. But I am not sure how far you will be able to follow!"

"Anyway, listening to You has always helped my heart to touch something not understandable."

Then with a face that glowed with gracious, gentle majesty, You began:

"Each individual is a spark of Spirit, apparently differentiated. The differentiation is only apparent – it is not real; yet these differentiations and divisions are infinite in number. Out of ignorance, each human being, although intrinsically a spark of the Spirit, asserts separateness, which becomes the personality. Each individual spark, on its way to realizing its oneness with the Spirit, develops a multitude of traits and behaviors which are regarded as characteristic of that specific personality.

"So instead of realizing its own true Individuality, the spark of the Spirit feels impelled to develop personality traits that it does not presently possess. In this way, the personality is continually either reformed or, unwittingly, deformed."

"Makes sense," I chirped up, although floundering already. "This seems to be a surprisingly deep subject."

Scarcely acknowledging my remark, You continued, "Eventually, due to satiation, which is rare, or anguish, which is more common, one wishes to break out of the prison of personality. When the identification with personality is weakened, there is the possibility of a door opening to the path of longing to realize one's true Individuality."

"So it seems necessary that I try to change my personality," I ventured. "But how?"

Eyes filled with loving compassion, You answered, "What is important is that while giving form to a so-called 'new personality,' you should be in a state of readiness to dismantle the earlier personality structure, if necessary, with its likes and dislikes. It takes real courage to do this, as there is a natural tendency to be satisfied with only small changes that impress and satisfy you, but which impede the inner flow of spontaneity that leads you to your real Individuality."

You gave me a probing look, as though to see how much of this I was grasping, and continued, "When you fashion and chisel the structure of a personality, regardless of how attractive and charismatic it may be to others, you must be ready to pull it down, even smash it. Beneath these ruins is your real Individuality.

"The idea of *becoming* relates to personality; that of *being* to Individuality. One may feel dissatisfied with one's personality and seek to change it, to become something else; people call it growth.

"In reality, there is neither being nor becoming.

The first, apparent, timeless becoming is the formation of 'dropness' in Me – the Ocean. Thus, the drop is one with the Ocean until the formation of an ephemeral bubble. This bubble goes on changing, and in the human form is referred to as 'personality.'

"This bubble creates the appearance of separation. It is a 'nothing' that appears to have substance. So the first becoming is the formation of a bubble over a drop. The final becoming is the conscious oceanness of the Ocean itself as Reality. All the innumerable, intermediate states of a bubble consist of the becomings of personality, which disguise the real nature of a drop as Ocean."

Radiating calm and majesty, You concluded,

> "The question is whether you wish
> to accomplish something
> or long to become nothing;
> to make a big splash in the ocean of falseness,
> or go deep, unseen and unsung,
> to find the pearl of Individuality."

My eyes did not wander once from Your countenance. Even in my confusion, Your deep, wondrous words were a light to my heart.

In spite of my incapacity, You were still in a mood for explanations; love overrules discrimination. You went on, "Personality is like a cage; individuality is like a bird perched within the cage. No matter how many changes are made in the shape and size of the cage, or the materials it is made of, the cage remains a prison for the bird. Yet these kinds of changes are not without purpose. The longing to soar freely in My immense expanse heightens one's perceptions and deepens the receptivity of the heart.

"Eventually, more and more bars of the cage, being bent again and again, begin to break, and a moment comes when the individual gives up the effort of reforming the personality, and instead surrenders to My Will. This leads to the final metamorphosis of personality into true Individuality. This is the state where the bubble totally disappears, as the drop merges in the Ocean, My Reality."

"I'm afraid this is all getting too deep for me!" I gasped. "I feel like I'm drowning!"

You laughed. "Then let us come to the surface. Let's go back to the clown in your story. He was on the verge of a very important realization: acting, whether in life or on stage, consists of wearing the clothes and faces of others. This kind of skill may amuse and enchant or lighten the stress of some people in an audience. But can such acting heal one's personal wounds or the agonies of an awakened heart?"

You gave me a compassionate look and asked,

"How long will you dress yourself in borrowed clothes? Isn't this a way of fooling others at the cost of deforming your own personality? Learn to take off these borrowed costumes, however bright and beautiful they may be. Cast them off and laugh at your foolishness for having clung to them for so long. This will initiate and speed the journey to find true Individuality.

"Thus, the process of reforming personality continues until personality is transformed into real Individuality, effortlessly manifesting the Will of My Reality."

Deeply engrossed, I closed my eyes and tried to touch what had seeped into me: Personality, Individuality, Reality; Personality, the changing bubble; Individuality, the enduring "drop"; Reality, the everlasting Ocean.

I remained withdrawn in contemplation until I felt You slap me on the shoulder. I opened my eyes to see You smiling at me with a look of amusement.

"Come back to your senses," You said. "And tell Me what became of that clown and the psychologist."

"I presume they're on their way to meeting You somewhere, sometime!"

You beamed with obvious delight. "That's right! Someday they must!"

The Perfect Timing

Your timing is of such perfection that no event ever occurs a moment prematurely. But knowing this is of little consolation when I'm suffering, and urgently praying for immediate deliverance. Not surprisingly, I am attached to my own ideas of what I think is right and essential, and of what, in my own particular case, constitutes perfect timing.

I was in this kind of state one day when I said to You desperately, "Yes, You are the most compassionate One, so why can't You be a little quicker in Your response to my cry?"

As I said this, I saw a look of pain flit across Your face. You answered me in a soft, subdued voice, "Don't you realize that I would like to be not only quicker, but to be the quickest of all, in answering your call? But I am not always able to do this."

"Why?" I asked, perplexed by the notion that there

was something, anything, You were unable to do.

"The sort of quickness you are asking for will not help you as it should," You explained. "It will not completely heal your wound. An abscess has to ripen and burst from within before the infection can be drained out. If a raw abscess is operated on in an untimely way, there may be some relief, but it will only be temporary. The abscess will reappear, causing greater pain than before. Isn't this true? In My love for you, I do not want to increase your pain even by giving you momentary relief. Or would you prefer it?" And You looked deep into my eyes, waiting to hear my answer.

"No, no, not at all," I stammered, anguished. "But what should I do when the pain is unbearable? I admit that at such times I lack trust in Your perfect timing, and this is why I cannot help but express my grief to You. To whom else could I say these things, if not to You?"

You responded with a look of deep intimacy and compassion. "Yes, you have to open your heart to Me. But then you also have to listen attentively to what I say and try to understand its meaning. Perfect timing is a mysterious process which becomes obvious to you only at its fructification. In fact, every moment is the culmination of a perfectly timed sequence that you are not aware of; there is no such thing as 'imperfect timing.'

Try to live the truth of this in your relationship with Me. Why don't you try?"

Whenever I recall these words, I realize that I have not yet surrendered my wishes to You, and that I have no courage to accept any calamity as one of Your attempts to save me from greater sufferings. Each dispensation of Your incomprehensible compassion is so unique and unprecedented that it baffles me. Frankly, I am helpless in this. Please be my guide and my hope.

You Alone Are Mine

I was not at all in good spirits. Certain doubts had begun to nag me, for I was beginning to distrust that which I had, up to now, trusted most. Skeptical remarks made by others about my relationship with You, which I had told myself repeatedly to disregard, had reduced me to this state. A mind can easily be overwhelmed by the immense diversity of people's perspectives about life, and I had proven susceptible to this.

Immersed in my anguish, I heard the doorbell ring. I went distractedly to answer it, and when I opened the door I saw You standing there, Your face full of anxious concern. You looked as though You had come in great haste.

It was an entirely new thing for me to see You looking so worried. But the love in Your eyes instantly gave me a feeling of security. I felt like a child who, having lost its mother in the tumult of a vast carnival, suddenly finds the hem of her garment again.

By the time we had settled ourselves, the characteristic glow had returned to Your face, yet my heart was plunged once again into a sea of turmoil and doubt.

In a warm, loving voice You inquired, "Why do you look so worried and woebegone?"

"Because of a wounded heart!"

"What has hurt you so deeply?"

"Well, a very serious matter has threatened the whole basis of my relationship with You."

"Yes, from your look and your words I can see it is something very critical. Why not share it with Me?"

And so I opened up to You. "There are people who say that what I write about Your visits is all imaginary."

"What's wrong with their saying this?" You asked mildly. "Are they not free to express their opinions? Why should this affect you so?"

"So You mean what they are saying is true?"

You answered matter-of-factly, "In a way, yes."

Your reply startled me; I could only stare at You.

You continued, "But at the same time, you must not forget that what others say is also a product of their personal worlds of imagination. Their opinions reflect the diversity of their relationships with Me, the Self-existent center within. So, you see, there are as many paths as individuals. Eventually, each one has to find one's path without being unduly influenced by the good or the bad in others. My help to you becomes more and more accessible when you decide to find and follow the path that is uniquely yours."

"I follow a little bit of what You are saying, but there are some who honestly believe that my experiences are just the delirious speculations of a weak mind."

You gave me a smile of gentle reproof. "But there are many, as You have told Me, for whom our dialogues are joyous and significant!

"Every truth in the realm of illusive imagination has an antithetical truth which appears to be equally true and valid. This is due to the inherent quality of all-pervasive Illusion. Everyone in Illusion is consciously or unconsciously seeking truth. Therefore, every perspective or idea, when honestly held, is valid, as it represents that person's search for truth. So one should remain open, or else one may become dogmatic and self-centered, ridiculing others, hurting their hearts. In one's journey to Me, there is an ongoing need to re-evaluate one's perspectives."

"So it seems I should not be so sensitive to these buffets, but rather take them as opportunities to strengthen my trust in You," I interjected.

"Right!" You looked happy. "I do not wish to take away anyone's freedom not to accept Me. If this nonacceptance is honest and strong, it has an even greater chance of helping them to feel My presence all the more. So you should not be influenced by what others say. I have My own ways of dealing with each of you. For Me, there is neither hurrying nor tarrying. Each will find their way to follow Me at the opportune time."

You had conveyed so many profound things that it left me breathless! I pondered for some moments before venturing, "So to think of You and remember You is the simplest way for an ordinary person like me to shed the veils of imagination to move closer to You, the Reality."

A benign tenderness came over Your face, and You answered, "My form is the purest, crowning aspect of Illusion, for it is directly linked with the Reality. Although, in the final analysis, My form is not real, yet it is the principal instrument for releasing anyone from the domain of Illusion. To give an analogy, My form can be likened to a very sharp thorn, which has a magical healing quality when used to draw out other deeply imbedded thorns in mind and heart. And when all those thorns are removed, this benign healing thorn, My form, mysteriously disappears, and one is totally merged in My formless Being.

"So remain totally unaffected by the comments of others, and follow without doubt what you hear Me say in your heart. The sound of My Name takes one to the real silence of Reality where My presence reigns. And My remembrance will guide you and lead you to the abode of Reality from which I come to visit you."

You gestured with a graceful sweep of Your hands and continued, "In Illusion there are wheels within wheels, and it is the 'master wheel' that turns them all. Each one is moving in its own world of imagination. Some are closely interconnected, but it is only My presence, permeating Divine Imagination, that touches them all. At a call from any heart, I take form to guide that one to My abode, which is beyond imagination. So My visits to anyone are specifically personal, but at the same time can be of significance to others. I am the Supreme Dreamer who appears in your dream to awaken you into My Reality."

My preoccupation had begun to diffuse, and I was ready to listen attentively. Your face illumined with divine authority, You resumed, "I am the one Reality, the everlasting, ever-renewing Spirit. Creation, My shadow, has come out of Me. It is My playground. So the Ocean of My Reality is in everything, in every drop, but it is covered by the ocean of Illusion. Each drop-self in creation has to find its real center and become conscious of the Reality, My Being. This is the purpose of My game in the playground of Illusion."

Though Your words mystified me, they conveyed

such a feeling of intimacy that I quipped, "Could You possibly be more abstruse?"

"Perhaps not." You smiled.

Your smile gave me the courage to add, "May I ask why You ever began this game, infinitely played in Illusion?"

"You will know why only after you have experienced the Reality. But you will not be able to explain it to anyone else." You smiled mischievously. "Maybe I would have withheld the creation, if you had been there to advise Me."

And then You grinned from ear to ear.

I marveled at Your descent from Your highest peak of divinity to respond to my foolish question with such playful humor.

You looked at me very sweetly and asked, "Are you satisfied? Is your heart convinced that My visits to you are real?"

I felt tears in my eyes, and with a choked voice answered, "Yes. I'm sorry for the clouds and doubts that for a while eclipsed my trust in You."

"Is the sky clear now?"

"Oh, yes."

"Then My mission is fulfilled."

"Most successfully!"

I had wanted to express my deep indebtedness to

You, but at that instant, You left. You never wait to hear a word of thanks; such is Your generosity!

Your words had poured liveliness and serenity into my faltering spirit, almost blinding me with their luminosity. However, a few streaks of Your light, touching my heart, projected themselves onto the canvas of my being:
>I am totally Yours,
>You alone are mine.

Bathing One's Being

One day I was taking a leisurely shower, feeling greatly refreshed, as I always do when I bathe. I had already soaped my face and body, and was reaching for the shampoo with my eyes full of suds, my head beneath the running water. My outstretched hand went slightly amiss; the shampoo bottle crashed to the floor, taking the soap dish with it. Reaching down, I momentarily lost my footing, my left hand shooting out to steady myself.

"Mercy!"

Lo and behold, the mishap was averted, but the bottle was cracked.

I finished my shower and wrapped a towel around my waist. Feeling very relaxed, I entered my room whistling, and saw You seated there – what a surprise!

"I've been waiting for you for quite a while." You smiled.

"Oh, I was having a bath," I said. "Sorry."

"No need to be sorry. People often think that I keep them waiting, but at least you won't say it."

"Or at least not always," I quipped.

Drying my hair in the mirror, I saw Your reflection, and asked impulsively, "Who combs Your hair? It always looks so soft, sparkling, and glistening with luster."

"Good heavens! Why don't you also ask Me what brand of shampoo I use!" And then You continued, "I am the ever-renewing Spirit. Every part of Me renews itself every moment."

I did not anticipate such a mischievous answer, playfully blending Your wit and wisdom.

Looking at Your countenance, I realized the truth of Your statement. You looked so sweetly resplendent: I felt that Your inner and outer beauty continually surpass each other.

"What brought You here?" I asked.

"Wait awhile. First comb your hair and dress yourself."

I hurriedly dressed myself, hung the towel back in the bathroom, and returned to the room.

I beheld You sitting there, so regal, yet in a state of total relaxation. Your eyes were closed, and an overwhelming silence permeated the atmosphere. I had never seen You with Your eyes closed. At that moment it was revealed to me that Your seeing is not dependent on Your eyes. You seemed to be fully alert, though absolutely motionless, so much so that for a moment I mistook You for one of the objects in the room. The next moment, it seemed as though each object was actually an integral part of Your presence. And then I felt that You were the center of everything, a circle without a circumference, a form without any periphery. How indivisible is Your presence! In the midst of my wonderment, Your eyes slowly opened and smiled into mine. Inwardly, I understood that You knew what I was thinking.

"I'm ready," I said.

"So am I," You replied.

"May I tell You what I thought just now?"

"Yes, of course."

"As I saw You when I entered the room, You looked so magnificent that I felt, 'How blessed it would be to die at this moment.' "

To my surprise, You looked displeased hearing these words.

"I fear I have made You unhappy," I said. "But why?"

"That you wished to die shows your mistrust in Me. Don't you believe that when that moment ordained by Me comes, I will be with you? Dying is living for Me, and in Me, with a smiling heart."

I felt ashamed of myself, and pleaded, "Don't be serious. I only expressed a feeling."

"It's okay. I too was doing the same."

"Fine. But now tell me what brought You here."

"Don't you remember calling Me when you slipped in the shower? The bottle was broken, but you escaped injury. I came when you called Me, and I waited for you here."

"I marvel that even an involuntary remembrance reaches You."

"But I am conscious even of your involuntary movements about which you are unconscious. By the way, do you know what real bathing means?"

"What's that?'

"Real bathing means washing mind and heart, through feeling My presence more and more intimately. Real bathing needs no soap or water; soap only washes the body, which soon becomes soiled again. Even a steam bath, which penetrates your deepest pores, leaves you susceptible to the pleasures of the senses. Cleansing the skin alone can only lead you to skin-deep love. Real bathing cleanses the heart and takes you closer to your real state of being."

"You mean that the act of bathing is more than just an activity in an enclosure; that it is an ongoing process of clearing away the mental darkness that covers the spark of life."

"Yes," You responded. "People like to feel smart and lively, as they often do after a bath, or after some sort of refreshing exercise. This feeling is like a renewal of the individual's resources. But then how are those resources put to use? Most often by seeking repetitions of sense pleasures, with small or great variations. Most people's idea of bathing is purely external and shallow. The quest for repetitions of trivial experiences spreads out and out, but never penetrates to a deeper level. Real bathing breaks through the inertia of these superficial fixations and takes you to a deeper level. It has a creative effect on your relationship with Me, the Living Spirit."

Listening to You, I slipped into a state of absorption, and You graciously allowed me some moments of quietude. Sensing that my heart was full, You then concluded, "My remembrance is the antidote for all the shadows of sorrow that cloud your life. It will transform them into positive energies. This will enable you to love life in its various aspects, without becoming attached, and to feel My presence more and more." You stood up, patted my shoulder, and said, "I won't keep you any longer. I know it's time for you to go to work."

"May I ask You just one question?"

"Not now." And You strode off as lightly and gracefully as though You had wings. I would have run after You, but something glued me to my seat. The intensity of Your visit, the sheer luminosity of Your presence, had pierced the veils of my illusory self. It took me a long time to orient myself to the so-called present. Your wish was that I attend to my work, and You were helping me not to displease You.

Silently I implored: "Let Your name flow through all my veins and flush away my selfish desires and thoughts, leading me to bathe in Your presence."

And a shower of Your tender, lively radiance drenched my being. An instant reassurance – amazing!

Let a Sip Be a Celebration!

It was past lunchtime, but I had no appetite. With eyes closed, I was quietly lying on my bed. The chronic bodily complaints had reappeared, and the mere mention of food brought nausea. Gripped with anxiety, I felt depressed, unbalanced. From these recurring symptoms and bouts of illness I felt physically battered and mentally shattered. While engrossed in this gloomy mood, I heard someone tiptoe into my room. As I opened my eyes, I saw You sitting at my bedside, Your face glowing with that ever-fresh smile.

    I hurriedly sat up. Casting a glance at me, eyes sparkling with endless vitality, You said, "What's the matter? What's wrong with you?"

    In a dejected tone I replied, "Nothing is right with me! How do I look?"

    "Well, your eyes look strained and your cheeks pale," You remarked.

Let a Sip Be a Celebration!

"Don't they tell You how I am?" I responded.

"Physically, yes. Chronic physical complaints often result in chronic deviation from the real center of life. So I was asking you, how are your spirits?"

"Frighteningly low!" I exploded.

"Why should you feel so? Haven't you yet learned that physical illness comes in the natural order of things and leaves the same way? It's a sort of tax you pay when temptations have led you to overestimate your capabilities."

"So this is a sort of punishment for me," I commented wryly.

"No. Don't take it that way; that would be disrespectful to the flow of life. It's a challenge to strengthen your relationship with Me. It's an opportunity, a time to regain greater poise and serenity; it can help you relax and detach yourself from the body and will initiate you in the life of spirit."

A bit startled, I said, "Then should I discontinue with my medical treatment?" But even as I said this, I knew the stupidity of my question.

However, without condemning or deriding me, You explained, "Don't be silly! Play your part well and that shall calm you down and also satisfy your mind. Your practical efforts to get over your sufferings will mellow you and help you to be sympathetic toward others. This process will reveal to you some precious aspects of human life. Suffering comes not to suffocate, but to put you in touch with deeper aspects of life."

You paused thoughtfully and then added, "Strive to feel that you are much stronger in spirit than what you take yourself to be. Be sure. And you are much weaker in flesh than what you think you are. Beware!"

"I am intrigued; how am I to judge the limits of spirit and those of my flesh?" I asked.

"Through constant awareness of your life itself," You replied. "With the passage of time, this attitude of witnessing, with detachment shall gradually take away the fear of the unknown and of death."

I hastily intervened, "What about the people suffering from terminal diseases, constantly facing death and needing reassurance on a deeper level?"

You looked at me with incomprehensible seriousness, yet also with great tenderness. "That is a question of an entirely different dimension. Let us not go into it today. However, know this much, that no one really dies, except to live in Me, forever."

You concluded, "Whether healthy or unhealthy, most people suffer from two common diseases."

"Which are these?" I asked impatiently.

"Worry and fear. And the two are finely interrelated. Worry is fears encapsulated and fear is worries activated!"

I broke in, "I am greatly affected by both of them; I do not know how to get out of their grip."

Calmly you continued, "You bring into existence whatever you seriously dwell on. At every moment, you have a free choice. So why entertain and project negative values? The more you desire the limited and limiting objects for the gratification of the flesh, the more you get away from the boundless, blissful life of spirit."

What You were asking of me was not easy, but Your words made me feel that You regarded my illness as Your own. Your intimate support filled my heart with courage. This made me bold enough to ask You, "But how do I get in touch with the life which You want me to lead?"

You smiled and said, "Simple. Begin knocking on the door of My spaceless mansion!"

"What!" I exclaimed. "That seems far, far away."

"No, it's very close, closer than your own breath."

"And yet farther away than the sky overhead!" I said, and together we laughed.

You continued, "Well, the distance is that which you create between your own doubts and your deep trust in My unconditional presence."

As we were conversing, the clock struck one. Pointing to it, You said, "Aren't you hungry?"

"Not really. Today I am going to take only a little broth."

"Then why delay? Bring the kettle here."

I stood up, but touched by Your love, my eyes brimmed with tears of joy, and I said, "Instead of taking broth from your hand, in fact, I wish to stay with You where time stands still. This shall free me for all time from physical maladies and mental depressions!"

Heavenly light shone in Your eyes. "You are always there with Me, yet on your own you swerve, and then *you* complain of being pushed away. Now, be quick and get your broth."

I went to the kitchen, brought the kettle, and placed it with a cup on a little stool. You filled the cup, looked at me from head to foot, and sweetly said, "In My remembrance, sip slowly the broth, with joy in heart and ease of mind, and My vital presence shall keep company with you. Give up despondency and don't worry."

While walking toward the door, You gave me a smile that filled my being with Your loving assurance. Entranced, I sat on my bed sipping the broth, and Your words became alive; I felt I was drinking life-giving nectar!

The sense of buoyancy that came from Your visit cannot be described in words, yet with the last sip, words flowed:

"All Glory to You!
Sometimes, as I sip, let it be a celebration
of Your glorious presence pouring into my heart!"

Was I asking too much of You?

"Remember Me Full-Heartedly"

There came a time when I was so overpowered by intense suffering that I stopped remembering You. But the moment I got a bit of relief I realized, through a flash in the heart, that You had been closer to me during that whole critical time than ever before. I cannot say how I knew this to be so, but I knew it nonetheless.

But what an irony! In spite of this knowledge, I felt a hollowness in my words of gratitude to You, a lack of whole-heartedness. All too quickly I became repossessed and consumed by the superficial charm and vanity of life. Now I found myself dealing with You like a worldly businessman, mechanically muttering formulae of thanks for services rendered. And I was disgusted with myself.

Then one day I stood before You, sheepishly raising my gaze to meet Your eyes, and the smile of Your forgiveness wiped away all sense of compunction. Your compassion is incomprehensible. I asked You to fill my heart with the assurance that You have accepted me as I am, and that I am Yours.

You relate to each individual in incomparable ways. No two of Your responses are outwardly alike. But in spite of differences of expression, every one of Your actions is saturated with the infinite concern for each individual. It is this diversity of expression, this fathomless and unpredictable renewal, that makes it difficult for me, at times, to see the underlying flow of Your compassion in present situations.

Our meeting that day was very brief, and at its conclusion, You rose to Your feet enveloped by Your silent splendor. Then You spoke for the first time, in a tone of gentle sweetness, "Try to remember Me *full-heartedly.* Real repentance means absolute trust in My continual forgiving. Accept this: and the acceptance will blossom in your heart in glorious ways. Be of good cheer. Don't be despondent; never fear, I am always with you."

Again I raised my eyes to meet Your gaze, but this time I found that I could not. Your acceptance of me was overwhelming. Instead, I found my glance had focused on Your feet, and I wished I could wash them with the tears of my gratitude.

A Cosmic Call

I

Even as I stepped into my room, Your vibrant presence had announced Your arrival. However, instead of greeting You, I first attended to arranging some trifles – odds and ends – that were cluttered in the corner. Then I turned to look at You.

But before I could say anything, You said, "That's good!"

Your words struck me, for they reminded me of the previous day's unexpected events. I responded, "Good morning," but also added, "Will You please let me know what made You say, 'That's good!'?"

You looked surprised by my question. "What do you mean? Isn't it a common expression? I simply expressed My appreciation about the way you keep things so neat and tidy."

"That's all?" I asked skeptically. "It just seems to me that there might be something deeper; please don't conceal it from me," I urged.

You raised Your hand and said, "Well, everything at one and the same time is natural and apparent. The secret is that, whatever the circumstances, any occurrence is an expression of My total response offered simultaneously on innumerable levels. Each happening has its own intrinsic logic, which may or may not be apparent at that moment."

After Your explanation, You smiled sweetly and said, "But tell Me, what prompted you to ask this question?"

Your meaningful words had made me thoughtful. But having noticed that You were in a light-hearted mood, I thought of sharing the related incidents of the day before. So I replied, "I have a very sound reason to ask why You said, 'That's good!', though others may not think so!"

"But why let your heart be influenced by what others think? I want you to feel free and open with Me about everything, whether the matter is petty or profound. This will help you to open your heart more and more to My light. For Me, nothing that is shared in love, with love, can be considered a trifle."

And so, encouraged, I began. "All right, here are

three ordinary incidents which seem to me to be mysteriously interrelated and also connected with Your first words to me this morning."

"Quick, I'm eager to hear this. Tell Me about them."

II

"Well, yesterday I biked to the countryside, and while passing a stream, I saw some flowers that looked splendid and fresh, swaying in the breeze, all delightful colors. Getting off my bike to pick some, I suddenly thought, 'Why should I disturb these flowers when they are having such a pleasant dialogue with the sun?' And instantly I changed my mind.

"Just then a flock of birds flew overhead, and their calls sounded like, 'That's good! That's good!' And I was reminded of Your words: 'Beauty is to be adored, not defiled; the beautiful are to be honored with no selfish interest.' So I threw a kiss to the flowers, and they seemed to wave back to me. The whole experience thrilled me in a very deep and personal way."

I stopped, waiting to see what Your reaction would be.

"Wonderful! What is the next episode?"

"Well, it was on the same day. On my way home I

had just turned onto a busy street when I spotted an expensive-looking leather briefcase lying by the curb. It had probably fallen off a luggage rack, and so I stopped to have a look. It had an address tag, and looking inside, I discovered there was quite a bit of money, as well as jewelry. Somebody had apparently gone off for a luxurious weekend. For a moment, the sight of all that money was tempting. I rationalized, 'Maybe this is a gift from You, coming to me without my asking for it.' But Your words, 'Be honest; I always provide before the real need arises,' came to my mind, and I got over the temptation.

"As it so happened, the address was on my way home. It was a very large, opulent-looking house. The owner of the briefcase had not returned, but there was someone there to take it, so I didn't linger.

"Getting back on my bike, I thought to myself, 'Your bounties are two-edged swords. They are neither to be used indiscriminately nor handled insensibly.' Just then a couple of people walked by, and I heard one of them say to the other, 'That's good! That's good!' I had no idea what they were talking about, but the words had a strong impact. Wondering, I watched them until they turned the corner."

I met Your eyes, and momentarily felt self-conscious. "I guess I could have left out some of the boring details."

"Not at all. These stories are quite interesting, and the little details, which some people call trivialities, are important. The more conscious one becomes of trivialities, the more one sees how they form a significant design. But come on, let Me hear the third story."

"I reached home in a very happy, meditative mood, thinking about the day's events. Although I usually read the newspaper or a magazine or book in the evening, I decided to clean the kitchen instead. While I was busy washing the cups and dishes, the tiny painted flowers on the crockery reminded me of the riverbank, and then I noticed that the flying birds on the sides of an old cookie jar seemed to be calling, 'That's good! That's good!' Somehow my mind seemed to slow down. Every little thing I did brought me joy. Nothing seemed insignificant or tedious.

"A while later I took a shower and turned on the television. An announcer was just wrapping up his account of the tennis final, and I heard the words, 'That's good! That's good!' This amazed me. Now I was really wondering about the successive repetition of this same phrase three times in one day. And when I turned to face You this morning, You said to me, 'That's good! That's good!' It seems incredible! Is this all just accidental?"

Your face glowed with enjoyment of my stories, despite their long-windedness. You asked, "What do you mean by 'accident'? Either everything that happens is an accident, or there is no such thing. Some people like to use the word 'miracle' for things that strike them as inexplicable. But there is nothing miraculous in any event, except as it may appear to an individual state of mind and understanding.

"Because you are influenced by intellectual explanations, you try to find reason and logic, especially in things that seem uncommon. There is nothing wrong with this, except for your assertive anticipation of finding a solution that will fit the strictures of your comprehension. This comes about because you forget that life is one integral whole, expressing itself simultaneously on numberless levels."

Your words often have a magical quality; on that day they poured a delightful silence into my heart. Your eyes met mine and filled my being with exultation. I lowered my gaze and murmured, "You are right, You are right," as though You needed any confirmation from me! "Still, I can't help feeling amazed by the reiteration of the same phrase in totally unconnected situations," I persisted.

III

Perhaps owing to my childish adamancy, You abandoned Your gravity and answered me with a look of merriment. "It's very simple; there's nothing complex or unnatural about it. When you call to one of your close friends who is some distance away, what do you do if he doesn't hear you or doesn't respond?"

"I call until I get his attention."

"Why?"

"Because of our friendship and mutual love."

Your smile shone even more brightly. "Then what is so remarkable about the same phrase being repeated four times?"

"So such recurrences form a meaningful pattern and have a special role to play?"

"Definitely. They express My intimacy and concern. You may even think of them as 'cosmic calls'! The logic of such events will silently manifest, often in ways which may appear to you as trifles – like the birds you heard calling the other morning. Whether great or trivial, the purpose behind each recurrence is to invite you, beckon you, to the Source of life that I am."

I drew in a deep breath. "It is impossible to listen to You without my heart being touched; then the profound depth of each of Your statements becomes apparent. Yet, strangely, a moment later I am apt to drown that drop of understanding in the ocean of my ignorance. And this happens again and again! I wonder what would become of me were it not for Your unconditional compassion!"

Just then, we glanced at one another, and I felt cool tears trickling down my cheeks. What caused them? Your reassurance? My own incapacity? Or both?

You consoled me, "Because of our relationship, you are always free to call on Me. I send you signals sometimes which can be totally new and unique, or they could be repetitions of My 'cosmic calls,' though perhaps in quite unexpected settings." And You laughed wholeheartedly.

"So there is hope for me," I managed to mutter.

"Not only for you, but for everyone, anyone. I am with you, in you, always, but I am more available in a most natural way when you call Me with love and trust."

"This means I have to keep You first and foremost in whatever I do, whether it is insignificantly small or astonishingly great."

"That's it; that's good!" You laughed, with a mischievous sparkle. And You rose gracefully and made Your way to the door.

I always feel delightfully alive and fresh in Your

presence. Don't ask me whether it is due to Your total humanity or absolute divinity. In fact, I do not wish to know. I fear that knowing the answer might take away the charm of our intimate relationship. Perhaps You will also agree with me on this point, and sweetly concur, "That's good!"

Influence, Presence, and Essence

I

Early one lovely morning, I strolled down the quiet lane by my house. The soft light of dawn was spreading across the sky. I had gathered a cluster of wildflowers, and as I walked I admired their enchanting colors.

In spite of feeling relaxed and refreshed from my walk, I found myself deeply preoccupied with some recent incidents which had made an impression on me.

A few days earlier I had gone to the circus. The highlight of the evening, for me, had been the acrobats, whose supple movements and superb positions and formations amazed me. I felt real awe at the spectacular coordination and agility of the human body, and thought to myself, "What a gift to be in the human form!" And then, a moment later, I asked myself, "But what is the purpose of it? What is it for?"

Another incident had to do with a lecture given by an illustrious scholar; again, I found myself amazed by a particular human aptitude – in this case, the fluent and easy manner in which the scholar was able to express the basic truths of daily living. And I had thought to myself, "Mind, with its faculty of rationality, is indeed an ingenious tool for understanding and discovery. From where does it draw its energy?"

A third incident: I had attended a program of devotional singing; the melody and rhythms of the songs giving voice to the various aspects of unconditional love seemed to pierce the depths of my heart. Without my being aware of it, tears trickled down my cheeks. "Why," I wondered, "does music have this incredible power to move the heart? Do tears help one to feel the pulse of the heart?"

And, finally, as I was nearing the end of my morning walk, I recalled a fourth episode. A friend of mine would often invite me to meetings of different groups of dedicated seekers of Truth. They introduced me to a number of techniques which seemed, at the time, highly effective, and made me feel that I had found my true path. But the feelings faded, and the experiences produced by the techniques did not last long.

Now, comparing myself with the various skillful, talented, erudite, and devoted people connected with these four events, I felt diminished and depressed. Compared with these giants, I was a pygmy. Within the ambit of conflicting claims relating to my body and mind, I felt a kind of grayness settle over me. And I wondered whether I would ever find a way in which body, mind, and heart could be brought into harmony with each other, so that the seeming gaps in my life's journey could be turned into bridges, and the achievements could become outposts inspiring me to go beyond them.

By the time I reached home, I was a mess of body, mind, and heart. But when I looked at my bouquet of common wildflowers, my spirits lifted, and I set about arranging them in a vase on my sitting room table. Just as I finished doing this, I was surprised by Your sweet, heartwarming voice behind me: "Wonderful! Marvelous!"

II

I turned and saw You standing in the center of the room, gazing intently at the bouquet with an expression of admiration and pleasure. There were no roses or lilies in the bouquet, just that random collection of wildflowers. But Your face radiated a subtle blend of pink and golden hues, and it seemed to me that creation's 'fairest flower' had come to visit me.

I couldn't guess what made You so happy. I simply stared at You, wordless, until You gave me a quizzical smile and said, "You seem to be deep in thought this morning."

I hesitated, but then confessed, "Yes, You're right. To be honest, my mind is all astir at the moment."

You showered me with Your smile, and teased, "So I suppose you have some questions for Me."

"Not a question, but a complaint," I retorted.

"Against whom?"

"Against no one in the world, not even the devil, but against You!" I exclaimed.

"Against Me? How could that be? Anyway, a complaint implies a series of questions." You smiled mischievously. "Being the Infinite One, at every moment I absorb complaints and shocks without number. What is one more complaint to Me?"

"I wish You'd be serious," I said. "My complaint is that You have created so many beautiful things and inspired so many human accomplishments in the world. I wish I could derive joy from them all, but instead I find they cause jealousy in me, and this has precipitated a real identity crisis."

As I concluded, You burst out laughing. "Identity crisis! That sounds very impressive! Do you know what it means?"

Influence, Presence, and Essence

I felt instantly deflated. I had been showing off with this imposing-sounding language. "I don't even know what I am, or what I should be," I said, somewhat nervously. "To make matters worse, I find myself envying others' talents, which are so much greater than my own."

Then I told You about the circus acrobats, the lecturer, the devotional singing, and the group meetings, and added, "Watching and listening to those talented people made me feel inferior and crave to emulate them."

III

"The trouble with you," You said, light-heartedly, "is that you have not made a proper distinction between appreciating others objectively and being unduly influenced by them. There is a fine line between appreciation and influence; the former is liberating and enjoyable, but the latter binds. It is by letting yourself be influenced that you rob yourself of the sweetness of what you see and experience."

"What do You mean by 'influence'?"

"Influence can sometimes imply a subtle comparison by which you measure yourself against others. Comparison might make you proud, but it can also make you feel depressed and lead to the agony of not accepting what you are. So try to see each thing's innate 'thingness,' and this will turn your envy into a receptive awareness of the beauty that resides in each thing for its own sake."

"This is really getting complicated," I interrupted. "Could You try to come down a little closer to my level?"

"Why only a little?" You replied. "Let us really come down to earth. It is said that on the equator any point at sea level is equidistant from the sun. Is that true?"

"I was never any good at geography, but I think it is true."

"Well, the same principle applies to My omnipresence, which abides in all, and is equally available to everyone. It is only your clouded perception that obscures this truth."

"Please help my mind and heart to understand a bit of what You are explaining," I implored, feeling a bit like a student who has fallen behind in his lessons.

With an expression of infinite kindness, yet at the same time looking at me quite pointedly, You resumed, "I mean to say that if you compare yourself with others and are jealous of their attainments, you will always complain and feel driven to emulate them instead of accepting yourself for who you are. The truth is that, ultimately, it does not matter what great things you have accomplished; real greatness of mind and heart is determined by what you have offered to Me. The more the mind is emptied of such thoughts as 'I have done this, I have done that,' the more your heart will fill with joy."

IV

"So You are saying that even small daily acts and responsibilities have a special value in my relationship with You?"

"The little ways of remembering Me can pave a path of sunshine for you. When offered to Me, those tiny responses from the heart – the common talks, the daily chores – can bring you joy. You will experience a feeling of lightness as the burden of responsibility for what you do devolves upon Me. Then these small exchanges and events will become great moments in your life. The important thing is not to be a clever talker, but rather to act with a pure and focused heart. But do not grow attached even to these rare and precious moments; if you release these moments by offering them to Me, you will find they grow in My presence. The human form with all its aptitudes and potential is a magnificent gift from Me. Treat it with the honor and respect it deserves by using your physical and mental skills with discrimination."

And You paused.

Your words had put my preoccupations to rest, and now a profound tranquillity came over me. I wanted to express my gratitude to You, but found myself unable to speak. At the same time, You seemed to be in an excellent mood, and a brilliant smile flashed from Your eyes.

In a loving yet cryptic way, You concluded, "My presence emerges from My Essence, the Reality that is beyond the Beyond."

Awe and wonder stirred within me, hearing this. "You speak of Your presence and Essence, but then . . . who *are* You?"

The next moment I felt the impudence of my question.

You didn't answer, yet Your expression seemed to grow more luminous, bathing my being with the radiance of Your compassion and forgiveness. Silently, You rose from the chair and moved to the vase. You picked out a single flower and gave it to me. At that moment, it seemed to be the most beautiful flower I had ever seen. While I stood there transfixed, You left.

Your departure didn't sadden me; rather, I was in a state of rapture. Gently, I returned the flower to the vase. To my amazement, every flower in the vase revealed itself to me in its own unique, exquisite splendor and the room was filled with a heavenly perfume. I remained enthralled by this vision for some timeless moments. Then I heard You speak in My heart:

"That flower was My gift to you, that your every thought, word, and deed may be your flower offering to Me, given in My remembrance. Let it instill harmony of body, mind, and heart. Then with My grace, and in My own time, you will know the answer to the question you asked Me." I heard Your chuckle, like the gentlest tinkling of bells. "And that will be the surprise of lifetimes . . . !"

Your words trailed off, but Your silent, blissful presence lingered.

Now I anxiously await that benevolent moment ordained by You. Until then, I pray that You bless me to resign myself patiently to Your blessed Will.

Not to sound impatient, but . . . will you?

Just for Nothing

Once I heard You say:

> "When you trust in Me, I wake up in you.
> When you are quiet, I speak through you.
> When you call on Me, I come to you.
> The more you depend on Me, the more I live with you."

So I asked You, "How can I feel this closeness with You? This is my problem."

You answered with a laugh, "Perhaps this is everyone's problem.

> "Innumerable are the ways to reach Me,
> each unique to each,
> each one holding a unique joy.
> In My infinity no two are alike.
> I offer help at every moment,
> but it often goes unnoticed.

> "I walk with you, but you find Me not;
> I talk with you, but you hear Me not;
> I am watching you, but you see Me not;
> I am ever with you, but you feel Me not.
>
> "It is not I who elude you,
> but you who veil yourself from Me.
> You ask Me for a clue –
> the secret is in your body."

"In my body!" I exclaimed. "How can this be?"
"Listen:

> "The very purpose of your body
> is to remind you of My presence.
> Your mind and heart function through your body.
> All external activities are oriented
> toward the internal journey.
> Objects of desire are craved
> to feed inner needs;
> the Center is within.
> And it is breath
> that links body, mind, and heart.
>
> "Slow, soft, rhythmic breath,

>   glowing, loving, lilting praise,
>   all in silence through thoughts and deeds,
>   a divine sowing and watering of seeds."

Deeply moved, I prayed to You:

>   "O Ancient One! Let Your Name rise
>   from the breath within,
>   and may Your grace ever guide me
>   to accept voluntarily and cheerfully
>   that every moment of my life
>   is a blessed gift from You."

You looked pleased, smiled, and said, "Just remember this simple 'Song of Nothing':

>   "The moment you get up,
>   remember Me for nothing.
>   When you go to bed,
>   remember Me just for nothing.
>
>   "When you leave your house, for a moment,
>   remember Me for nothing.
>   When you come home, just for a moment,
>   remember Me for nothing.

Just for Nothing

"Before you have breakfast,
remember Me for nothing.
When you finish your supper,
remember Me just for nothing.

"Remembering Me for nothing
will relieve your stress and tension.
Remembering Me for nothing
will renew your heart with courage and cheer.
Remembering Me for nothing will enliven
your thoughts and deeds with heavenly music,
and I will be the conductor of
the symphony of your life.

"Remember Me in the beginning,
remember Me in the end,
I will take care of the in-between.

"When you remember Me for nothing,
you expect nothing from Me.
This will prepare you
for My real response to each moment,
and you will catch the spirit
of the game I play with you.

> "In this 'nothing' you may find
> the seeds of everything you need.
> Isn't it simple?"

"Perhaps too simple!" I said.

"When I give you deep and profound explanations of life, you complain, 'This is too profound; it's beyond me!' Now I have shown you a simple way, and you say it is too simple!"

You gave me an intimate, reassuring look:

> "Trust Me: don't be nervous, don't be anxious.
> Keep going, and be happy in My remembrance."

The Book

I wrote just one word, "Speak," put down the pen, and began to laugh. I had wanted to write about what happened to me during a week when I attempted to follow one of Your guidelines. This entailed recording a series of failures, some highly comical.

A filmic procession of these episodes now flashed across the screen of my mind. I couldn't contain myself. I cradled my face in my hands and sat there helplessly laughing.

Just then there was a pat on my shoulder. Startled, I opened my eyes, turned around, and beheld You standing behind me, Your face lit with a winsome smile.

"What's so funny?" You asked.

"You are the cause of this!" I said, trying to compose myself.

"Well, I know I am the Primal Cause of all, of

everything, but what is the specific reason for all this laughter?"

So I began to explain, "You see, I had resolved to follow one of Your guidelines for just seven days and . . ." Again, I broke into laughter.

"And what?" You prompted.

"Well, I must admit that I failed miserably. But it was also amusing to find, later on, how with each failure Your words came back to me, pointing out my mistakes. And I would see how I had lied for nothing, how I had unnecessarily exaggerated many things to show myself off. . . ."

I was about to go on enthusiastically narrating more of my failures, but You stopped me. "Which guideline, specifically, are you referring to?"

"Oh, sorry. I forgot the main thing. It was a short, five-word saying that You told me once: 'Speak only when you must.' And was it ever fun trying to put this into practice!"

You smiled and said, "So your attempt to become an honorable silent sage turned you into a chatterbox!"

"More or less," I admitted. "How I'm grateful to You for Your words. They kept bringing to my notice how often I would poke my nose into things that were none of my business, and how frequently I had offered unsolicited advice where it was of no interest. I could see how my own verbosity had prevented others from expressing their views. In various ways, You showed me what a windbag I really am, wasting energy and breath for nothing, playing at conversation as though it were a game in which to excel and prove myself."

I went on spewing forth a hodgepodge of observations about myself and my experiences, and then, becoming self-conscious, concluded: "But believe me, I tried earnestly to follow Your advice."

And I waited for Your reaction.

"Don't be surprised if you come to find that most of your words were mere chaff," You replied. "To converse well is to know well when not to speak. But when You speak in a spirit of humility, in an effort to understand and communicate with others, this is not a waste of energy. If you are trying to bring a smile to an unhappy face, or if you are singing praises glorifying Me, this is as good as observing silence." You paused, and then asked, "But what do you mean by the word 'earnest'?"

" 'Earnest' means being sincere," I answered. "It means being serious, conscientious, about whatever one is doing. Doesn't it?"

"You're just quoting the dictionary. Is that all the word means to you?"

"Well, this is what I learned in grammar school. If it has another, deeper meaning, please tell me about it."

You looked probingly at me. "In a certain sense, being earnest means more than just being conscientious. It also means becoming more and more aware of My being with you in your journey to Me, through the various levels of ignorance. Your quest should be to find what really exists, the Reality. For this, you have to get rid of the attitude of 'I am doing this, I am doing that.' Instead, you should try to feel that whatever activity you are engaged in is being done by Me through you. You should just be an instrument for Me to express My love for you in all the different aspects of life."

My blank expression undoubtedly revealed my lack of comprehension. You cast a gracious glance at me which touched my spirit and intensified my awareness.

Then You continued, "Listen carefully: The feeling of 'I am doing this, I am doing that' is generated by your 'I-ness,' which is like a lead weight pulling you down into the pits of egoism. But if you make Me the doer, your burdens will not only be lightened, but will become wings raising you to the realms of My light. At present, your thoughts and activities are rooted in 'I-ness.' This 'I-ness' serves a necessary purpose, holding all your diverse experiences into a cohesive whole. This 'I-ness' can be likened to the thread in a garland."

"But if I lose that thread of 'I-ness,' won't I become hopelessly disoriented?" I asked nervously.

"That's right," You replied placidly. Then, seeing my distress, You smiled gently. "That is what *would* happen but for My companionship and compassion. By making Me the center of your life in everything you do, it is possible to transform the thread of 'I-ness,' bit by bit, and yet the garland remains. As you become more willing and proficient in this, you will find that every time you give this thread of 'I-ness' an earnest tug, it acts as an invitation to Me. Then the 'I-ness' you disown is transformed into a beam of My presence."

"Your simple simile makes sense to me," I responded, "even if only a little!"

"Good!" You looked genuinely happy that I had absorbed at least a small part of Your explanation. "Whatever you do, do it wholeheartedly, but without claiming the results as your own, whether good or bad. Then the responsibility for your actions devolves on Me. You must long to lose your 'I-ness' and become more and more aware of My presence flowing continually in you and through you."

The discussion had moved to too high a level. "This is all very enlightening," I said. "But I'm afraid it's beyond me."

You understood my helplessness and immediately changed Your tone. "Well then," You said cheerfully, "what else would you like to talk about?"

"I don't know. My head is still spinning. I would like to understand the deeper levels of life and, more than that, to really live them by discarding 'I-ness.' Your words sparkle with such refreshing clarity, blending profundity and simplicity. But just now a thought is knocking on the door of my mind with some urgency."

A look of amused suspicion crossed Your face. "Are you leading up to some special question? If you are, go ahead and ask."

So I opened my heart, and my mouth, to You. "Actually, I have been wanting to ask You something for quite some time."

"What?"

"I would like to request that You write a book. There should be some chapters elucidating the theme of Life, followed by some important guidelines. I'm sure that such a book would enlighten many people and help them with their problems. Wouldn't this make You happy?" I said all of this in one breath, lest You skillfully distract me.

You chuckled. "But my dear fellow, don't you know that I have already written that book?"

"Don't make fun of my suggestion. I really mean it."

"I'm telling you the truth."

It was hard for me to believe what You said. You

read my look of skepticism and added, "You are free to think what you like."

"Then let me know the title of the book," I rejoined, thinking to catch You.

You answered in a clear, even tone, "*Heart Speaks*, and it is placed in each individual's heart. Isn't that a good title and a good place to keep it? What do you think?" And You winked at me.

Fumbling for my answer, and at the same time trying to play along with Your joke, I replied, "I will grant that You have delivered the book right into my heart, but You have not given me the sight to read it!"

"When longing becomes intense, then, of itself, it turns into an eye, and the words of the book become visible to it. Gradually, the eye of discrimination and the eye of intuition will open, and you will be able to read the book, *Heart Speaks*. And slowly your 'I-ness' will be transformed by earnestly offering your thoughts, words, and deeds to Me, and you will experience that I am ever more present in your life."

With deep gratitude I said, "So what really matters is that I try to be aware of You being the only doer, and that I learn to lean on You more and more to release me from my 'I-ness,' while doing everything, anything, anytime." I looked imploringly at You. "I am sure You will help me in my earnest efforts. Please prepare me to

act as Your instrument, but don't make it too difficult!"
And I smiled.

This seemed to please You. You stood up to leave. In mute adoration I gazed at You, and our eyes met. Before leaving, You placed Your hand over my heart. What joy came over me at that moment, I cannot describe! Was this gesture clearing a direct path to my heart where the "Book" of love and light waits to be seen and read?

Then it came to me that this "Book" is not meant to be read, but to be listened to and felt in one's heart. Its script is longing, and its language is love.

Heart Speaks!

The Bill Unpayable

Injured by false allegations circulated by an intimate friend of mine, my mind was plunged into turmoil. I was greatly annoyed with myself for not being able to deal with the situation. The gossip had been going on for over a month, and had become unbearable for me.

Disillusioned and dejected, I threw myself into a chair. How close we had been, and yet . . . Sadly I closed my eyes to block out the sorry spectacle of this world.

Then I heard a soft voice. "Are you angry, or are you meditating?" You asked.

I opened my eyes to see You there. "Both!" I fumed.

"Angry meditation! This is something new! But what happened that made you lose your temper?"

"Something I really did not expect," I grumbled.

"The unexpected is always waiting around the corner, and one should be ready to face it without losing one's equilibrium." And again You inquired gently, "What is troubling you?"

"Accusations that are totally false!" I exploded.

"If the charges are really false, why should they affect you?" You asked mildly.

"But there are so many deceitful rumors that accompany them! What has become of my image in society!"

"You should have been more concerned about My image in your eyes than about your image in the eyes of others," You cautioned. "Eventually the truth shall prevail."

But I was too aroused to be appeased by this kind of assurance. "What should I do until then?" I snapped. "Just keep my mouth shut about all of this?"

"Well, not necessarily, if you can't wait. But regardless of what you say or do, you shouldn't lose your mental balance because of it. In fact, you could have taken this unexpected experience as a challenge to face the situation cheerfully." And You smiled.

I was still smarting and unable, or perhaps unwilling, to relinquish my sense of indignation. "How I wish I could do that. But it's too much! Impossible!"

"Yes, you could be right," You sighed. And then You suggested, "Why don't we take a walk in the park? The open air, the blue sky, the sparkling leaves and flowers will help you calm down. Get your hat, but don't look in the mirror." You winked at me.

I gave you a borrowed smile, and responded, "I know my face is red with anger."

We went to a quiet, beautiful spot in the park, but I was oblivious to the loveliness that surrounded me. The subject of our conversation still weighed on my mind. Impatiently, I asked, "What did You mean about accepting all of this as a challenge to be cheerful?"

"Here we are in such a beautiful, buoyant atmosphere, and you still haven't left your room. Come outside," You urged. "Be here for awhile."

"But first," I insisted, "tell me why all of this should have happened."

"Because I wanted to get a rise out of you."

"Get a rise out of me! Why?"

"So that some nonsense buried deep within you could be brought to the surface and wiped away."

"But how am I supposed to know that it is You doing these things?"

"I can give you simple clues, but it may not be easy for you to follow them."

"Tell me, I'll try to understand."

"The people you live and associate with are the masks that I wear over My innumerable selves. Through the mutual responses and reactions that you experience in your life, I help you to discover this truth. So some even call Me the 'Mask Master.' What do you think of this name?"

By now Your presence and Your words had softened my mood. "Your masquerade is so perfect and profound, and the unmasking so difficult, that it would be more likely for people to call You the 'Task Master.'" And I smiled.

You seemed pleased that my spirits were lifting. "Aside from what other people may say or think, how would you prefer to address Me?"

Suddenly a feeling of gratitude came over me, and I answered spontaneously, "As the 'Perfect Doctor' who knows the cure for anyone's wounded spirit."

"So you're feeling better now?"

"Yes, definitely."

"Then you'll have to pay the Doctor His fee."

"Send me the bill," I rejoined.

"It will come soon."

"I'll be waiting."

And both of us laughed.

Just about then a crowd of people began to drift our way, and so we parted.

In a bright, happy mood, greatly relieved, I reached home. There was an envelope on the table. I could recognize the handwriting as that of the friend who had created all of the uproar with the defaming rumors. I wanted to tear it to pieces.

But something within prompted me to open the letter. The contents greatly surprised me:

> . . . totally misinformed . . . deepest apologies...terribly sorry. Let us be friends again. Please forgive me and also all of those involved in this unfortunate incident.

I could scarcely believe what I was reading. It was hard to absorb. And the thought flashed through my mind: "Is this the 'bill' You promised to send me, that I am to forgive all of these people?"

The next moment all of the misery and bitterness I had experienced over the past few weeks welled up in me once again. All of those caustic remarks rang in my ears; I saw the sarcastic expressions. Yet, as I saw those faces in my mind's eye, it was as though You were winking at me through their eyes. "Cheer up! Clear up the bill! Now is the time."

"But does merely saying 'Sorry' mean truly feeling sorry in one's heart?" I asked myself. Real forgiveness seemed far beyond me. The wounds that were still bleeding in my heart were not willing to say "Forgiven" so readily; in fact, some were moaning, "Why forgive? Is this fair?"

"This bill is unpayable," I mumbled to myself. My inability to keep my word to You brought tears to my eyes. Slowly I pulled out a chair and lowered myself into it. What was being brought to the surface, and what was being wiped away? I had no idea. Nevertheless, I felt that what You had told me had deep significance. I did not need to know it, but only prayed to You, "Please help me pay Your bill."

The Gifts

"May I ask You something?" I inquired shyly.

Your gracious eyes rested on me, and You smiled. "Have I ever visited you without your asking Me something? When are you going to be done with all these questions?"

"Only when I begin to listen to You continually in my heart," I said, beaming triumphantly.

You raised Your eyebrows. "A clever reply."

"I do not wish to be clever," I rejoined. "Please don't make me clever. I would rather be an ordinary person who can open his heart to You without hesitation, on any subject, great or small, anytime."

"So! You have something serious in mind today. All right, then, what is it?" And, abruptly, Your look of amusement became one of concern. "Is something troubling you?"

"Actually, yes," I confessed. "Not always, but often

enough. Your use of that word 'clever' reminded me of it just now. There are times when I can't help but worry about the gifts You have bestowed upon me. I know that I shouldn't, but sometimes I can't help myself."

"I don't understand," You said, with apparent innocence, yet with a twinkle in Your eye. "Don't you like My gifts?"

"It isn't that! I am more than happy with the gifts You have given me. But sometimes I'm apprehensive. Perhaps I feel unworthy of Your gifts, or that I may lose them."

This explanation felt lame to me, and I broke off.

You looked penetratingly at me, and asked quietly, "Am I not free to withdraw that which I have freely conferred?"

"Of course You are totally free. But what really frightens me the most is that if I lost any of Your gifts, I might also lose my gratitude for having received them. And by 'gifts,' I mean gifts of all kinds – a healthy body, talent, a special ability. . . ."

You stopped me with a gesture of caution. "To cling with a sense of attachment to My gifts would be to confine oneself within that which is meant to give free expression to life. It is to prevent this kind of limitation and rigidity that, sometimes, I withdraw the gifts I have bestowed. I do this in order to renew them. So it is for you to freely and happily use what I give you, and for Me to give and take freely, as I choose. By trying to retain and possess these gifts as your own, fearing their loss, you obstruct the flow of My grace within you."

I couldn't help but interrupt You at this point. "I just don't understand where these fears come from!"

You resumed patiently, "When you feel that your accustomed patterns of life and the joys you derive from them are being threatened, you are alarmed and begin to worry. Fear and worry rob you of My presence, and this, in turn, intensifies them all the more. You begin to fume and fret, obstructing the process of renewal. In such a state, how can you realize the blossoming of My presence within you? Or would you rather that I withheld those deeper gifts which will bring you closer to Me?"

"My dependence on You is my only strength, and my relationship with You is the deepest concern of my life," I answered earnestly.

"Then become a trustee, a keeper, of My gifts. If you think that you have earned and own them, you will be liable to claim credit for them and expect recognition from others. This kind of self-glorification can begin without your being aware of it, and eventually can block My gifts and their regeneration and transformation. Understand, renewal is growth, and growth is My response to the inner needs of your being. Growth can be painful at times, but I want you to know that with every pain of growth and maturation, I am with you."

A glow of compassion lit Your face, and it seemed that a soft divine radiance encompassed Your entire form.

"I am truly grateful to You for everything," I said. "But in spite of that, the pain of renewal frightens me. Something within me always holds back, clinging to the way things have been. Forgive me, but the idea of drastic change has always scared me."

Your look of intimate concern returned. "Why should anyone resist a transformation when it is the natural outcome of an ongoing process of growth? By lovingly accepting the inevitability, the naturalness, of what I want for you, your trust in Me will increase. Accept the passing painful moments, and You will be amazed by the healing energy that is released within you. It will reinitiate the true adventure of your heart, and My grace will sustain you unfailingly."

Your voice deepened, became more resonant, and my sense of wonderment increased, as You intoned:

> "Every moment is a sea of bliss;
> every leaf a glorious, refreshing song.
> But it is your conditioned awareness
> that hides you from the innate charm."

The Gifts

The golden rays of Your smile washed over me, that astounding shower of compassion, by which, again and again, You stoop to my level to impart Your love to me.

I felt a prayer escape my lips in a whisper. "Let Your joyful remembrance and my willing acceptance of both the bestowal and the withdrawal of Your gifts be constant in my life."

"Take heart," You answered gently. "Talent and excellence are gifts from Me, and if such gifts are withdrawn or changed, it is because of My compassion and is meant to keep you spiritually trim and fit. Complacency and inertia confine My gifts; when you accept change, trusting Me, you will be freed again, and you will feel My presence in your heart all the more."

"I can understand that I should accept Your wish, even though I often find that my wishes run counter to Yours. But . . . may I say frankly what I feel?"

"Of course," You replied. "When have I ever wanted you to do otherwise?"

"Whenever I go through periods of change, I feel the loss of Your presence. This is what troubles me."

"The problem is that you confuse My presence with the conditions in which you feel it. You confuse the wine with the wine cup. Life is a constant flow to reach Me. If unpleasant memories of the past or fears of the future cause you to cling to My gifts, then the joy of the present – the ongoing flow of life – will be lost."

"Yet it is so difficult to avoid the shadows of the past or the dark clouds of the future."

"Try coming directly out into the sun. Time is one 'indivisible present' in which My presence continually blossoms. Life itself is My gift to you, slowly unfolding this marvel. The ability to perform exceptionally in any field is a gift from Me. But one of the greatest gifts is the ability to witness, silently, life's unfolding to reach Me. In intense witnessing, the acceptance of 'what is' is without resistance; so My response becomes deep and profound. You have only to witness, and this, in itself, will bring you closer and deeper into My presence, ever shining and beckoning you from the heart."

I was silent for a while, as the simple immensity of Your words sank into me. Then, glancing up, I saw that look of amusement in Your eye again. So I quipped, "Why didn't You tell me this in the beginning?"

You chuckled. "Because then we would have missed the grace and charm of this conversation, and you would not have understood the nature of the real gift! Remember Me in all ways and remain happy always. This will guide you to the everlasting and ever-renewing sea of inner bliss – the Gift of gifts."

An enthralling smile blossomed in Your eyes, filling my being.

Inseparable Are Your Name and Form

I
Reflection

Through both Your name and form,
Your presence equally reveals itself as Love;
for Your name and form are inseparable.

Innate in Your name is Your form,
Inherent in Your form is Your name.
This awareness infuses something blessed into
    life,
giving nectar to every name and form.

This interplay of name and form
creates such a perfect blending
that at times You appear as name without form,
or just form which cannot be named.

Does this blending rise up from the bottomless
   depths,
or descend as grace from above? Who can say?
But it transforms Your name into form
and Your form into name, this much can be
   said.

Your name and form originate in one another,
and merge again in Your unfathomable silence.
You are the manifested One, the silent One
Who sows and nurtures the specific name or
   form
which is most naturally accessible to everyone.

Once awakened to this gift of grace,
the heart begins to sing the song of love to You,
glorifying the ocean of beauty contained in You.

Assuming a form that takes a name
provides Your love an excuse
to draw us into Your shoreless Being
where Your presence radiates infinite hues.

II
Transition

When that spark – the embryo of Your eye –
assumed Your form, it
consumed the numberless forms
to which I was helplessly attached.

And the first syllable of Your germinal name
as it coursed through my breath
softly cleansed the obstructions in my veins
ushering in the flow of Your presence.

May that spark become insatiable,
and that name become unutterable,
until the totality of Your presence
permeates every name and form I hear and see.

III
Conversation

Yet what an irony that my mind – my friend –
instead of seeking Your pleasure
often attempts to weigh the pros and cons
to find what is most easy and beneficial.

So I asked You, guardedly, "What is profitable?
What is greater – Your name or Your form?"
You looked deep into infinity
and seemed to reflect for some moments.

And as I looked at You, I felt
waves of pink and gold flowing from Your eyes;
and splendid forms gracefully
emerging and merging back into that radiance.

Then You smiled comfortingly at me and replied,
"When My name seeps into the unconscious realm of mind,
it strums the sweetest chords of the heart.
And when My form becomes the source of your sight,
it reflects itself in other forms with a graceful start."

And You concluded,
"So the song that sings the glory of either
name or form is equally great!"

In Your loving consideration for all
I have noticed that You remain ever noncommittal.
So I smiled back faintly and said, "Yes, I know."
Meaning I would never know!

Your all-encompassing answer
is an unfinished, unfolding art,
ever guiding one and all
to You, the Radiant Heart.
Then You looked deep into my eyes
and rose up, saying:
"Wholehearted remembrance of My name or
　form
releases My unconditional benign presence.
And in this is the answer to everything,
to any question, in the real sense."

IV
Confession

I do not live what I write;
what I write I live not.
But what a consolation – You signed on my
　heart!
Even *me*, a nonsensical naught.

And this made me sing, and carry
to every part of my being, Your message:
"My name is 'Love for the sake of love!'
My form is 'Compassion for the sake of nothing!'"

What a compassionate Love
and loving Compassion are You!